An Introduction Coping with Anxiety

**Brenda Hogan and
Lee Brosan**

ROBINSON
London

Constable & Robinson Ltd
55-56 Russell Square
London
WC1B 4HP
www.overcoming.co.uk

First published in the UK by Robinson,
an imprint of Constable & Robinson Ltd 2007

Important note
This booklet is not intended as a substitute for medical advice or treatment.
Any person with a condition requiring medical attention should consult
a qualified medical practitioner or suitable therapist.

ISBN: 978-1-84529-278-2

Printed and bound in the EU

11 10 9

Contents

About This Booklet

Most of us feel anxious at certain times in our day-to-day lives – for instance when we feel scared or threatened by a situation and think that we may not be able to deal with it effectively. Taking an important exam, going to a job interview and making a public speech are some of the situations people often describe as anxiety-provoking. Usually, as the situation passes, the anxiety drops. While everyone feels anxious at times, for some of us anxiety can seem unbearable and unmanageable.

For some people, anxiety never seems to go away, even when there are no real problems to face. And some people experience such extreme anxiety that it begins to interfere with their daily lives and they feel they just can't cope any more. This can be confusing and frightening, and they may start to worry that it will never get any better.

This booklet will help you understand what's going on when you feel anxious. Part 1 describes the symptoms of anxiety and explains the way in which these are kept going. Part 2 then gives you practical skills you can use to combat the symptoms of anxiety in three important areas – your physical symptoms, your thinking and your behaviour. By understanding and learning these key skills you can turn your problems with anxiety into things of the past.

It's often helpful to write things down, and Part 2 of the booklet describes several exercises for you to do, with completed examples to guide you. It's a good idea to get a notebook before you begin to work through these, so that you can keep a record of your thoughts, feelings and progress as suggested in the various exercises.

Good luck!

Brenda Hogan and Lee Brosan

Part 1: ABOUT ANXIETY

1 So What Is Anxiety?

Sitting an exam, going for a job interview, meeting future in-laws, having to make a complaint at your child's school – all of these situations may make you feel anxious just by thinking about them, and dealing with the actual event can be a major ordeal. You may feel threatened or frightened. When we get anxious we become aware of a range of emotional and physical symptoms including:

◆ feeling nervous, anxious or frightened
◆ heart beating faster (or heart 'flutters')
◆ shortness of breath
◆ sweating
◆ trembling
◆ muscles tense up
◆ dry mouth
◆ feeling sick
◆ 'butterflies' in the stomach
◆ feeling light-headed
◆ tingling sensations in the hands and feet
◆ strange things happen to vision

Feeling anxious can make life miserable. You can end up worrying too much, going over and over the worries in your mind, and finding it simpler just to avoid or leave situations that are likely to cause you anxiety. However the symptoms are entirely *normal* – and sometimes even useful. Read on to find out why.

Being anxious makes you think in a different way

Sometimes when I worry I feel really awful. My worries go round and round in circles in my head and I start to worry that I won't be able to cope. The more I worry, the worse I feel – I feel anxious, on edge and tense. Sometimes it gets so bad that I can't sit still.

Anxiety is a mixture of emotions, from feeling nervous or frightened, to experiencing panic or terror. A certain level of anxiety is normal – everyone has these moments – and even useful as it makes us pay attention to situations that may be dangerous. If our ancient ancestors hadn't felt anxious about coming face-to-face with a sabre-toothed tiger, they might have walked straight into its jaws. In modern life, anxiety still keeps us safe – for example, feeling nervous as you stand at the edge of a cliff makes it more likely that you will take a step back and less likely that you will fall off. Or you might feel anxious about walking home late at night along a dark alley, so you take the well-lit, perhaps longer route instead – this is good sense and means you are less likely to be mugged.

So some anxiety is normal and necessary, even though we don't enjoy the sensation. It helps us avoid potentially dangerous or harmful situations.

Being anxious has a physical effect on you

> *I start getting hot and sweaty and my mouth gets really dry. My heart pounds in my chest. Sometimes I even find it hard to breathe. The worse I feel, the more I want to run away . . .*

Most people have heard of the **fight-or-flight response**. This is a physical response that occurs in alarming circumstances – your reaction will either be to fight or run for your life. This is our bodies' safety mechanism allowing us to respond quickly in an emergency and our bodies release a chemical called adrenalin which triggers lots of physical changes:

- breathing faster to increase oxygen in the body
- faster heart rate to increase blood flow to the muscles
- more tension in muscles for a quick response
- less saliva, causing a dry mouth
- trembling or shaking
- sweating to cool the body down
- mind focusing on the source of the threat

Most of these changes will make us better at fighting or running away. For instance, increased blood flow to the muscles makes us stronger or faster. This survival mechanism has evolved over millions of years to protect us from danger and can still be very useful to us today – we can act fast to jump out of the way of an oncoming vehicle or to run after a small child who is just about to walk in front of a swing in the park.

However modern life is rarely dangerous on a physical level. If your boss criticizes you or if you have to give a presentation at work, running away or fighting is not very helpful! Many of today's situations that make us feel anxious and do not require a physical response – rather we need to *think* about a practical solution.

In some cases these physical changes are necessary and helpful. But as we have seen, sometimes it is a mental response that is required rather than a physical one. The unused physical activity in your body can be very distressing, but it may help to remind yourself that at least they are normal.

Being anxious affects the way we think

> *When I hear a rattle in the car I start worrying right away. I can't sleep because I'm thinking about what might be wrong and I'm worried about how much it will cost.*

Anxiety affects the way we think about things. As you've seen earlier, one part of the flight-or-fight response was 'mind focusing on the source of threat'. When you're in real danger, it's clearly sensible to focus on the source of the threat – you wouldn't want to ignore a car hurtling towards you as you cross the road! But some people react in the same way to situations which are not at all threatening or dangerous, or they over-estimate the true level of danger. When this happens, their bodies go into fight-or-flight mode, and they feel anxious even when the situation is relatively safe. Some people are always looking for possible sources of danger which increase their anxiety. For example, they worry that things will go wrong even when there is no reason to believe that this will happen – like worrying that the alarm won't go off even though it has never failed before or worrying that a family member driving a long distance might get in a car accident even though that person has a clean driving record and drives long distances quite frequently – this kind of worrying almost always leads to feelings of anxiety.

Some people feel that anxiety is interfering with their lives. When this happens, people often complain that they 'worry all the time'. They worry about 'anything and everything' and feel as though their worrying is out of control. It's hardly a surprise that all this worrying increases their feelings of anxiety.

Although worry and anxiety are similar, they are not exactly the same (see p. 12).

Anxiety affects our behaviour

> I used to really like having friends over for a meal. But then I started getting worried about getting everything "just right" . . . I would spend days planning the food and cleaning the house, and I would worry so much that it spoiled the fun. After our friends left I would worry about whether they had really had a good time. So I just stopped having people over.

So anxiety can change how we lead our lives.

Many people avoid situations that make them anxious – they may stop going to parties where they don't know many people or they go but leave early if they begin to feel nervous. Other people use 'safety behaviours' – for example they may stay close to a friend or family member or always offer to help in the kitchen when faced with a social situation that makes them feel anxious.

Avoiding situations that make you anxious and using safety behaviours are common – and they work, but *only in the short term*. In the long term, people find it even more difficult to deal with their anxieties because this way of behaving gives you false messages, such as 'the only reason nothing terrible happened is because you didn't go' or 'the only reason you coped was because you sat in the kitchen all night' or 'you got out just in time'.

Avoidance and safety behaviours lead to more anxiety and make it more difficult to face similar situations in the future. Also, your list of safety behaviours and avoided situations grows longer and longer.

2 Anxiety's Vicious Circle

Unfortunately, the different aspects of anxiety – emotional, physical, thoughts and behaviour – work together to form a vicious circle of anxiety. First, for example, let's imagine that you are about to give some sort of presentation at work but you're worried about speaking in public. Second, this thought makes you nervous, which triggers the 'fight-or-flight' response, so you feel short of breath and shaky. Third, you'll probably think that everyone will now see how nervous you are and they'll know you're not up to it. This, of course, will increase your nervousness. Fourth, the physical response will then get stronger, which will make you worry even more, producing a vicious circle like the one below.

ANXIOUS THOUGHT
(They'll think I'm no good)

PHYSICAL RESPONSE
(Breathless, shaky)

Many treatments of anxiety are now based on a successful method known as cognitive behaviour therapy (CBT). This method teaches you how certain ways of thinking are actually causing the anxiety by giving you a distorted picture of what's going on in your life, and helps you weaken the connections between the situations which worry you and your anxious reaction to them. CBT suggests that it is the first part of this vicious circle (the anxious thought) that is most important in producing anxiety. If you tend to see things as threatening and dangerous, and imagine that the worst will happen, then you are very likely to feel anxious.

When you are feeling anxious you may be affected by all four parts of the vicious circle (emotions, physical responses, thoughts and behaviours), or you may only notice problems with one or two. To work out what causes the most problems for you, ask yourself the questions below.

Emotions

◆ Do I often feel anxious, nervous, or edgy?

Physical symptoms

◆ Do I suffer from any of these symptoms: racing heart, shortness of breath, light-headedness, 'butterflies' in my stomach, trembling or dry mouth?

Thoughts

◆ Is worrying a problem for me? Do I feel that my worrying is out of control? Do I worry about 'anything and everything'?

Behaviour

◆ Do I avoid doing certain things because they make me feel nervous or worried?

◆ If I start to feel nervous in a particular situation, do I try to escape as quickly as I can?

◆ Do I avoid doing things by myself because I feel more comfortable when someone else is with me?

◆ Do I use 'tricks' to try to feel less anxious or to disguise the fact that I am anxious (for example, making sure I stay close to someone I know, avoiding eye contact or playing with my mobile phone)?

Although it may seem impossible to change how you feel it can be done! Because all four parts of anxiety work together, if you work on changing one area, it will help with the others too. So by making changes to how you think or behave, or to how your body reacts, you can make big changes to how you *feel*. In Part 2 of this booklet we show you how to do this.

Part 2: COPING WITH ANXIETY

3 Managing the Physical Symptoms of Anxiety

Most of us find the physical symptoms we described in Part 1 unpleasant and difficult to cope with. The following exercises are specifically designed to help reduce the feelings caused by anxiety.

Over-breathing

You've probably noticed that your breathing becomes shallower and faster when you are very anxious – this is called 'over-breathing'. Sometimes this will be very obvious, but some people don't realize that their breathing has changed. It's not dangerous to breathe more quickly and shallowly – it's similar to the way you breathe when exercising – but if you breathe like this when you are not exercising, you may have some uncomfortable side-effects, such as dizziness or feeling 'faint', tingling in the hands or feet, and your vision may seem distorted.

Oddly enough, one side-effect of over-breathing is that it can make you feel as if you're not getting enough air. Trying to breathe *more* will actually make the symptoms worse, not better. Again, it is not dangerous to breathe more, but it will result in temporary discomfort.

A good way to counteract the symptoms of incorrect breathing and to reduce the physical symptoms of anxiety is to use the **Controlled Breathing** technique.

Controlled breathing

When you first try this exercise, lie down, or sit in a comfortable chair. As you become more experienced with controlled breathing, you can try it sitting upright or standing.

1 Place one hand on your chest and on your stomach.

2 Breathe in deeply and slowly through your nose, allowing your tummy and chest to swell gently. Look down at your hands. Is your lower hand moving? Good. This means that you are using all your lung space, not just panting from the top of your lungs. Ideally, you should see gentle movement in both your top and lower hand. If not, try to push your tummy out very slightly as you breathe in. This will encourage breathing from the whole of your lungs.

3 The in-breath should be slow, gentle and quiet – no one else should be able to hear you breathe.

4 Hold the breath briefly.

5 Breathe out, slowly and gently.

6 After breathing out, pause for a moment. Don't take the next breath in until you feel it is 'time'.

7 Repeat this process. Try to get a rhythm going. Keep the breathing slow, deep and gentle.

Tense muscles

Relaxation techniques can help you calm down and lower your overall level of anxiety. Below, you'll find a set of instructions for **progressive muscle relaxation**. Read them through a couple of times before starting. (You might find it easier to record the instructions onto a tape so you can play it while trying the technique.) Try the exercise at least twice a day at first and allow yourself about 30 minutes (it probably won't take that long, but you don't want to feel rushed, so allow yourself a bit of extra time). Choose a time when you are alone and not expecting interruptions, unplug your phone and switch off your mobile! Sit or lie down in a comfortable place. It helps if the room is restful, warm and pleasantly lit. Try not to worry about whether you are 'doing it right'. The most important thing is to give it a try.

Progressive Relaxation

1 Find a comfortable position with your arms resting loosely at your sides, legs uncrossed. Be still for a few minutes to help you get into the right frame of mind and let yourself start to unwind. Take a couple of deep breaths. Focus on your breathing, and let your muscles slowly relax.

If you feel uncomfortable, change your position at any time – you don't have to worry about staying completely still. If your mind wanders during the exercise bring your attention back to your breathing.

2 Now roll your neck gently from side to side to loosen your muscles. Raise your shoulders up to your ears, hold them there, and then drop your shoulders. Let the weight of your shoulders fall gently back down. Focus on your breathing. Breathe slowly and gently, in through your nose, and out through your mouth. Let yourself relax. Imagine that each time you breathe out, you let go of some of the tension.

3 Now turn all your attention to your **feet** and how they feel. Tighten the muscles by raising your feet up a little bit, and pointing your toes towards the ceiling. Feel the tension in your feet, toes, and calves. Notice the tension and tightness in the muscles. Hold this for about 5 seconds and then let it go. Relax. Let the tension melt away to be replaced by a wave of relaxation. Concentrate on the changing sensations in your muscles as they move from a tense state to a more relaxed one. Relax your feet and toes. Focus on how that feels, as you gently breathe in and out. Focus on the feeling of relaxation for about 20 seconds.

4 Now tighten the **hip and leg** muscles by pressing down on your heels. You should feel tension in your calves and in your upper legs. Focus on that tension and the tightness. Hold it for about 5 seconds, and then relax. Feel the tension draining out of your legs, being replaced by a comfortable feeling of relaxation. Imagine the muscles smoothing out, becoming soft and relaxed. Focus on the relaxation for about 20 seconds as the tension just slips away.

5 Now for your **abdomen**. Tighten your tummy muscles as much as you can. Suck in your tummy and hold the tension. Focus on the tightness and tension for about 5 seconds. Then relax – allow the muscles to go limp and loose. Let the relaxed sensation spread slowly and gently over your abdomen. Keep your attention on the feelings of calm relaxation for about 20 seconds.

6 The next step focuses on your **chest muscles**. Take a deep breath in though your nose. Hold it. Feel the tension around your rib cage. Hold it for a moment, and then let it go. Breathe out gently and slowly. Feel the changes in your chest as you breathe out.

Breathe in deeply, filling your lungs, hold it, notice the tension, and then release it, breathing out through your mouth. Let your chest muscles relax. Return to slow and gentle breathing. Focus on the feeling of relaxation.

7 Now turn your attention to your **hands** and **forearms**. Place your hands palm up. Squeeze them into fists as tightly as you can, and turn the fists towards the ceiling. Feel the tension in your fingers, palms and forearms for about 5 seconds, and then let go. Slowly and gently, let your hands and arms relax. Let the relaxation spread over your arms, hands and fingers as the tension drains away. Remember to focus on the relaxed feeling for about 20 seconds.

8 Now for the rest of your **arms**. Create tension by pressing your hands down as hard as you can feel the tightness and tension. Hold it for about 5 seconds, then let it go. Let your hands rest gently and comfortably. Allow the tension to slip away. Focus on the relaxation in your arms for about 20 seconds.

9 And now try to tense all the muscles in your **neck** for about 5 seconds, then relax. Let your head rest gently, and let the muscles relax, becoming soft and smooth. Feel the tension slipping away, and feel yourself relaxing even further.

10 Now take a moment to focus on your **shoulders**. Notice any tension already there. Then tense the muscles by shrugging. Pull your shoulders up towards your ears, as if there was a string pulling them up. Hold the position for 5 seconds, noticing the tightness and tension. Then slowly relax, letting your shoulders gently drop back down. Focus on relaxing the shoulder muscles. Focus on the feeling of relaxation for about 20 seconds.

11 Move your attention to your **mouth** and **jaw**. Tense this area by clenching your teeth and pulling your mouth into a forced smile. Your lips, cheeks and jaw should feel very tense and tight. Hold it for about 5 seconds and then relax your face. Feel the muscles loosen and become soft. Allow your teeth to part and the muscles to soften and relax. Let the relaxation spread across your jaw and mouth. Remember to focus on the feeling of relaxation for about 20 seconds.

12 Now move up to your **eyes** and **nose**. Close your eyes as tightly as you can, and wrinkle your nose. Feel the tension in your face, your upper cheeks and eyes. Focus on the tension for 5 seconds. And then relax. Notice the tension slipping away. Imagine your muscles becoming smooth and relaxed. Focus on the feeling of relaxation for about 20 seconds.

13 You have now reached your **forehead**. Raise your eyebrows as high as you can. Notice the tension and tightness in your forehead and scalp. Hold it for 5 seconds then let go. Feel the relaxation spread back from your forehead, all the way across your scalp, for 20 seconds.

14 You have now gone through all the muscle groups in your body. Continue to relax, and each time you breathe out, allow yourself to become even more relaxed. Each time you breathe out, think of a part of your body, and then allow the muscles to relax even more.

15 When you have completed the relaxation exercise, take a moment to let yourself become more alert. Open your eyes, and move your arms and legs around a little bit before you get up and start being active again.

When you first try this exercise, you may find it difficult to relax your muscles, or you may have trouble concentrating on relaxing. That's why it is important to practise the techniques – it takes time and practice to be able to relax effectively. If you practise twice a day, you'll start to notice that it takes you a shorter time to relax. When you feel ready, reduce the amount of time you spend practising and use your skills whenever you feel you need them. With practice, you'll become more aware when your muscles are tense, and will be able to relax them 'on-the-spot'. Use this technique whenever you feel yourself getting nervous.

Too much caffeine

Your body reacts to caffeine in much the same way as it reacts during the fight-or-flight response. So too much caffeine will make your anxiety feel much worse.

Caffeine is in coffee, tea (including green tea and some flavoured teas), cola (and some other fizzy drinks – check the ingredients list to be sure) and chocolate.

Think about how much of each of these items you consume daily. It's probably more than you think, so might want to keep a 'caffeine diary' for a few days to keep track.

Caffeine is addictive, so the more you have the more you become dependent on it. Your tolerance of it will increase – you'll need more caffeine to get the same effects – and you'll experience withdrawal symptoms if you don't get it. Common withdrawal symptoms include headaches, tiredness and shakiness, as well as a strong urge to have a cup of coffee or tea! So if you are drinking a lot of caffeine, you may find it quite difficult to go 'cold turkey' and stop having it. To avoid the unpleasant withdrawal symptoms reduce the amount of caffeine you drink *gradually*. The good news is that you don't have to cut it from your diet completely. Small amounts of caffeine – a cup of coffee or tea in the morning – do not have a major impact on anxiety levels. Decaffeinated drinks are a good alternative.

Cut caffeine out completely in the late afternoons and evenings if you're having problems with sleeping.

4 Anxious Thoughts and Worrying

Generally, when we talk about 'anxiety' we mean the whole picture – thinking, feeling, physical changes and behaviour. When we talk about 'worry' we are referring to the thinking part of anxiety. You've probably noticed that when you are anxious, you think about things in a very different way from when you are relaxed. Things that normally wouldn't worry you may seem like total disasters. You may find yourself thinking that 'everything will go wrong' or that you will be unable to cope. You may even find yourself worrying about things that never bothered you before, like why your partner is 10 minutes late back from work – has he or she been involved in an accident? Or is that cough you have really a sign of a serious disease?

People who are struggling with worrying tend to think about things in very extreme terms. For example, they believe:

◆ It is *very likely* that things will go wrong.

◆ When things do go wrong, they will go *dreadfully wrong*.

◆ When things do go wrong, they will be *unable to cope*.

This way of thinking is likely to make anxiety even worse. People who 'get stuck' in these thought patterns find themselves in a vicious circle. The more you worry the more anxious you feel. And the more anxious you feel, the more you worry.

Worrying

Anxiety

The trick here is to break the circular link between worrying and anxiety. Although this sounds difficult, you *can* learn to change the way you think, and see things in a way that is much less likely to make you feel anxious.

5 Identifying and Challenging Anxious Thoughts

Just two steps can help you successfully challenge worrying thoughts and make them a thing of the past. First, you have to recognize when you are worrying and work out which thoughts are making you anxious. Second, you need to replace those thoughts with fairer and more realistic alternatives. We show you how to achieve these steps in the following pages.

Identifying thoughts that are making you anxious

This can be difficult as you may have become so used to worrying, and the thoughts may be so quick and automatic, that you don't even notice you are having them! So whenever you start feeling anxious, pay very close attention to what is going through your mind at that moment.

You may have thoughts such as 'I can't cope' or 'What if I screw up?', or you may have mental pictures, such as an image of a car accident or yourself doing something embarrassing. Both kinds of thoughts can cause high levels of anxiety.

Keeping a 'thought record' of situations that make you feel anxious and what you're thinking when you feel your anxiety rising can be a useful tool. To do this, first write down what you were doing when you started to feel anxious. Then ask yourself what you were *thinking* about when you started to feel anxious. (If it was an image, describe it.)

Finally, write down how you felt – your emotions. Anxiety isn't the only possibility. For example, you might also feel nervous, panicky or impatient.

Here is an example of a **thought record**.

In a notebook, or on a piece of paper, copy the headings in the example below and use this form to keep track of anxiety-provoking situations, your thoughts and your emotions.

Situation	What was I thinking about?	How did this make me feel?
Friend cancels lunch plans	Why did she cancel? Maybe she is angry with me.	Worried, anxious
Meeting at work	My work isn't good enough. Everyone will think I'm useless. What if I get the sack?	Anxious, panicky

TIP

Sometimes anxious thoughts are like 'flashes' and happen very quickly – without you paying much attention. For this reason, it's best to think about anxious thoughts when you are anxious. If you wait until you have calmed down, you may not be able to remember exactly what you were thinking.

Challenging the thoughts that make you anxious

What you then have to do is work out whether this is really the most realistic way to think about things, or whether there is a more balanced alternative. Worrying thoughts are very often biased and based on guesses and exaggerations, rather than on facts. Learning how to think about the same situation in a more balanced way can help you break the vicious circle of anxiety so that you feel less anxious and better able to cope with difficulties.

At first it won't be easy to challenge your worrying thoughts. The technique of **thought challenging** (see below) is a tried and tested way to help you do this. This can be difficult at first, but the more you practise this, the easier and more 'natural' it will become.

To develop a more confident way of thinking, ask yourself these five questions:

◆ Are there any good reasons to be so worried?

◆ Are there any good reasons not to be so worried?

◆ Is there another way of looking at this?

◆ What is the worst that could happen?

◆ What can I do about it?

We discuss each of these questions in more detail below.

Are there any good reasons to be so worried?

When answering this question, ask yourself:

◆ What are the facts of the situation?

◆ Do the facts support what I think or do they contradict it?

◆ Would somebody else think my thoughts were based on facts?

Are there any good reasons not to be so worried?

Now ask yourself if there are any possible reasons why you should *not* be having this thought. Your answers to the first questions might give you some clues about why you don't need to be so worried. Another way to do this is to think of things that happened in the past that contradict your current worry. Or try to remember times when you worried about something similar and were wrong. You can also try asking yourself these questions:

◆ Am I jumping to conclusions?

◆ Am I predicting the future?

◆ Am I guessing what other people think?

◆ Am I overestimating the probability of this happening?

◆ Will this problem matter in one week/one month/one year from now?

Is there another way to look at this?

Whatever you are worrying about there is almost always another, more helpful way of looking at the problem. But when you're anxious it can seem impossible to see the wood for the trees. Another person's point of view may be helpful here – so ask yourself what someone else, perhaps a close friend you admire, might think in your situation. Alternatively, consider what you would say to a friend in a similar situation.

The alternative thoughts you come up with have to be realistic – if they're not, you simply won't believe them. You should think about the pros and cons for the alternative viewpoint in order to decide whether it is more realistic and helpful than the original thought worrying you.

What is the worst that could happen?

Anyone struggling with anxiety probably thinks about bad things happening in the future. These thoughts can be very disturbing, so you 'push them out of your mind' without thinking things through carefully. But you need to confront these thoughts and ask yourself, 'What is the worst that could happen?' This may show that:

◆ Your worst fear is so exaggerated that it is *extremely unlikely or even impossible.*

◆ What you fear may be *much less likely* to happen than you previously predicted.

◆ Even if what you fear *does happen*, you may be *able to cope with it better* than you originally thought.

Once you've worked out what your worst fear is, ask yourself: 'How likely is it that this would actually happen?' This may be all you need to put the thought into perspective. It can be even more helpful to take it a stage further and ask yourself: 'How would I cope if this did happen?' Don't underestimate yourself. You probably have past experiences and personal skills that would help you cope in difficult situations (see below).

What can I do about it?

Ask yourself:

◆ Have I dealt with similar situations or with other stressful situations in the past? What did I do then that could help me now?

◆ What skills or abilities do I have that might help me cope with the situation?

◆ What advice would I give a friend who was in a similar situation?

◆ Who can I turn to for help, support or advice?

◆ Do I have all the facts I need? If not, how could I find out more?

You need to ask yourself what you can do in the immediate future to deal with the situation, and work out a specific plan. If you think you might benefit from some help with problem-solving, have a look at that section in this booklet (see p. 29).

Below is an example of the way thought challenging works. In your notebook, copy the five questions below and use them to practise identifying and challenging your anxious thoughts. Remember, the more you practise, the easier it will get.

Thought challenging in action

Anxious thought: 'I have to present the results of the project I've been working on. My supervisor will be critical and disappointed in my work.'

Are there any good reasons to be so worried? My supervisor has been critical before, but she is critical of everyone.

Are there any good reasons not to be so worried? I worked hard on the project and finished it on time. I did a pretty good job. I worried about a similar situation a few months ago and everything turned out fine. My supervisor has praised my work in the past. My colleagues have said that I work hard and that I'm competent. I think that I may be overestimating the chances of my supervisor being critical.

Is there another way of looking at this? Maybe my supervisor will be satisfied with the report. Even if she has some criticisms, it won't mean that the entire report was a failure.

What is the worst that could happen? She may think the report is rubbish and I will lose my job. Realistically, I think it is very unlikely that I will lose my job over this. It is unrealistic that she will think the report is rubbish. If I did get fired, I would look for a new job. I have lots of experience, so it shouldn't be too difficult to find one fairly quickly.

What can I do about it? The report is done now, so there isn't much to do but wait. If my supervisor is critical, I will make some changes to the report. It will be important to think about her criticism rationally and not blow it out of proportion. It may also be a good idea to talk to my colleague Sally if I feel stressed so that I can get her perspective.

6 Negative Beliefs About Worrying

So far, we've been looking at worrying thoughts about *situations*. But in recent years, psychologists have identified another aspect to worry that can be described as 'worrying about worrying'. If this is your problem and you tackle it, you could feel a great deal less anxious.

Some people have strong beliefs about the negative effects of worrying. They often fall into one of the following categories:

I'm worried because my worrying is 'out of control'

You may be plagued by thoughts such as 'I can't stop worrying' or 'My worries are going to take over and control me'.

I'm worried that worrying is harmful

You may be thinking: 'I could go crazy with worrying' or 'It's not normal to worry' or 'If I keep worrying, I will have a nervous breakdown' or 'If I keep worrying, I'll have a heart attack'.

If you're afraid that your worrying is out of control or harmful then you are likely to worry more, not less. This will make you feel more anxious, and you will therefore worry more – yet another vicious circle. Like other worries, these thoughts tend to be biased and based on exaggeration, and are not helpful.

If this is how you are feeling, read the following sections and try some of the practice exercises.

I'm worried because my worrying is 'out of control'

If you feel as if your worrying has completely 'taken over' your life, you may believe that there is very little you can do about it.

But let's consider this in a bit more detail. Think about what it's usually like when you are worried and anxious, then ask yourself the following questions:

♦ Do I eventually stop worrying?

♦ Can I think of times when something happened (e.g. the phone rang) that interrupted or stopped the worry? What happened?

♦ Can I think of times when I did something (e.g. turned on the television or made a cup of tea) that interrupted or stopped the worry? What did I do?

♦ Have I ever succeeded in stopping myself worrying by distracting myself?

Now that you have thought more carefully about your worrying and your ability to stop worrying, it's a good time to note your conclusions. For instance, you may have realized that you don't actually worry *all* the time and that you are able to interrupt your worry sometimes. This shows that you have more control than you thought over your worrying. Look at your answers to the above questions and then ask yourself: 'What does this show about my control over worry?' Write your answer down.

The problem with trying to 'control' your thoughts

Most people would agree that as soon as you try not to think about something, you think about it even more! So a distressing thought becomes even more persistent and troubling.

You can prove this point by doing the following experiment:

For the next two minutes, do not think about a pink elephant. Do not let the thought or image of a pink elephant come into your mind.

What happened? Most people who try this experiment say that they had difficulty *not* thinking about a pink elephant, or that an image of a pink elephant kept popping into their mind. It is extremely unusual for someone to say that they did not think of pink elephants at all.

So, what happens when you try not to think about a worry, or try not to think about something that might trigger a worry? Rather than helping you to *not* think about it, these attempts make it more likely that you *will* start worrying, or that you will keep on worrying.

In other words, trying to force the worry out of your mind and just 'stop thinking about it' actually makes it pretty certain that you *will* worry. Annoying though it is, the sad fact is that the more you try to stop thinking about something, the more you do think about it. And what's more, this will probably convince you (wrongly) that your worrying is indeed out of control. What you need is a strategy that is less likely to make the problem worse, such as **controlled worry periods**.

Controlled worry periods

To use controlled worry periods, follow these three simple steps:

◆ As soon as you notice that you are worrying, *postpone it* by telling yourself that you will allow time to worry about the problem later in the day.

◆ Choose a time in the day when you will give yourself 15 minutes to worry (preferably not in the hour or two before bedtime).

◆ When this time arrives, allow yourself to worry for 15 minutes and no more (set a timer if you need reminding!). Only spend the time worrying if you still feel it is necessary to worry. If the problem doesn't seem important any more, don't spend time worrying about it.

Postponing your worries is different from trying to suppress or ignore them. When you postpone a worry, you are not telling your mind to stop worrying. Instead, you are asking your mind to move the worry aside for a little while so you can focus on other things. Later, you will allow your mind to come back to the worry.

Use controlled worry periods for one week and see what happens. Then consider what you have found. Write down in your notebook, or on a piece of paper, the heading 'Proof that Worrying Is Controllable', and list all your discoveries. This might include statements like: 'I am sometimes able to stop worrying', or 'When I keep busy, I don't worry nearly as much', or 'When I use controlled worry periods, I spend much less time worrying during the day'. You can use this list as a reminder in the future.

I'm worried that worrying is harmful

Many people who have long-term problems with anxiety are troubled by thoughts such as:

'It's not normal to worry – there must be something wrong with me.'

'Worrying may make me go mad or have a nervous breakdown.'

'Worrying may cause a heart attack.'

Thoughts like these make your anxiety even worse. It's very important to confront them so you can think more realistically about the effects of worrying.

Let's begin with concerns about whether worrying is normal or not.

'It is not normal to worry – there must be something wrong with me.'

Worrying *is* normal. Most people say that they worry, and, at some point in their lives, they find worrying distressing. In fact, it would be virtually impossible to find an adult who claimed that he or she *never* worried.

Do you find this hard to believe? If so, it might be a good idea to find out for yourself whether the people around you spend time worrying. Try the following experiment.

Ask four people – two people that you think may spend some time worrying, and two that you think don't worry at all (or don't worry very much) – whether they worry.
Have they ever worried 'too much' about something?
When was the last time they found themselves feeling worried about something?

Name	What they said about worrying
Joanne	She worries that her boss thinks she's not good at her job. She worries that she may be sacked. She sometimes worries that her boss knows she's worrying about ...

You may be surprised at what you discover! Think about the responses that people give you, and what this new information tells you about worrying being normal.

Based on this information, write down a fairer and more helpful description about how normal it is to worry in your notebook.

Keep reminding yourself about this, especially if you find the old concerns creeping back. Remember that changing the way you think about things takes time and practice but you can do it.

'Worrying may make me go mad or have a nervous breakdown'

Remember that almost everyone worries sometimes, and that most people say that worrying has, at some point, been distressing for them. Does this mean that most people have mental health problems? Of course not. Worrying is clearly normal and is not a sign of mental illness or breakdown.

Can worrying lead to a mental breakdown? The answer to this question is 'no'. It is true that it can make you feel tired and very unhappy, so you may *feel* as though you are about to crack up, but in fact *this does not happen*. The stress caused by worrying does not cause mental breakdown either. Our ancestors lived in conditions that were much more stressful than the conditions we face now. So if stress caused mental breakdown, humans would never have survived as a species.

Think about times in your own life when you were very worried and anxious? Perhaps you were taking your driving test, or had to give a speech at a large wedding. What happened? Did you have a mental breakdown? No.

Using these facts, write down in your notebook a more realistic thought about the effect of worrying on mental health.

'Worrying may cause a heart attack'

Can worrying cause a heart attack or damage your body in some other way?

The physical symptoms of anxiety can be quite uncomfortable and you may worry that anxiety is 'doing damage' to your body. However, remember that the physical symptoms are part of the fight-or-flight response (see p. 6) and are intended to activate our bodies for defence. This response is normal and healthy, if a bit uncomfortable.

There is no proof that anxiety causes heart attacks. Many of the physical symptoms experienced when we are anxious are very similar to those we have when we are exercising. This isn't surprising when you consider that the fight-or-flight response is really just your body preparing you for physical exertion. And we know that exercise is healthy and is even recommended by doctors!

Now write down in your notebook a more accurate comment about the effect of worrying on physical health.

Thinking about worrying in a more helpful way

Now read over everything you have written supporting the fact that worrying is normal and not harmful. Think about any proof for and against the belief that worrying is harmful. Based on this proof, you can sum up a more helpful way of thinking about worrying in a chart like the one opposite.

Now it's your turn. Copy these two column headings at the top of a new page in your notebook. Underneath them write down your original negative thoughts about the effects of worrying and then use your new knowledge to come up with some fairer and more helpful thoughts about the effects of worrying.

Negative thoughts about the effects of worrying	Fairer and more helpful thoughts about the effects of worrying
Worrying is not normal.	Worrying is normal – everyone worries sometimes.
Worrying may cause mental breakdown.	Worrying does not cause mental breakdown – it is a normal and is not harmful, even if it does feel horrible.
Worrying may cause a heart attack.	Worrying will not cause a heart attack. Feeling anxious is a normal and healthy part of being human. My heart may be pounding, but it also pounds during exercise.

You may need to repeat this exercise (and the exercises shown earlier in this section) whenever you find yourself 'worrying about worrying'. Remember that changing the way you think about things takes practice.

Even if you don't quite believe what you are writing, put it down anyway. Some ideas take some getting used to, and you will find that the more you look at the new ideas, the more believable they will seem, and the less realistic the old ones seem.

7 Positive Beliefs About Worrying

So far, we have talked about how to deal with negative ideas about the effects of worrying. But it is also quite common for people to believe that there are *positive* effects to worrying. This is why some people find it so difficult to 'give up' worrying.

Common positive beliefs about worrying are:

◆ Worrying helps me solve problems.

◆ Worrying helps me cope.

◆ If I worry, I can prevent bad things from happening.

◆ If I worry, I will be prepared.

Ask yourself these questions: 'Do I think there are any advantages to worrying?' and 'Are there

any reasons why I shouldn't give up worrying completely?' Write down your answers in your notebook.

Unfortunately, these beliefs can convince you that you *should* be worrying. And, not surprisingly, this can lead to you worrying even more. It is very important to consider whether you think about worrying in a positive way, and if so, weigh up the evidence for and against these beliefs. In the next section we show you how to do this.

We're now going to suggest how you can examine your thoughts about the positive effects of worrying and develop a fairer and more realistic way of thinking about the usefulness (or uselessness!) of worrying.

The advantages and disadvantages of worrying

Start by weighing up the advantages and disadvantages of worrying, as we have shown in the box below.

Advantages of worrying	Disadvantages of worrying
Worrying helps me cope.	Worry makes me anxious and miserable.
If I worry it will help me prepare in case the problem really happens.	I spend too much time worrying – it's a waste.
	My worries are often unrealistic. Most of the time the things I worry about don't happen. Worry probably isn't helping me prepare – I think I would handle the problem in almost the same way if I didn't spend any time worrying beforehand.

Now try filling in a chart like this for yourself. Just thinking about and listing the pros and cons like this can help you realize just how many disadvantages there are to worrying.

Weighing up the evidence

Focussing on why you hold certain beliefs about the positive effects of worrying can be a useful exercise. Ask yourself the following questions:

◆ Do I have any evidence for my belief?

◆ If so, could there be an alternative explanation?

◆ Do I have any evidence against my belief?

◆ Can I think of any times in my life when I did not worry and events turned out positively?

◆ Does worrying really prevent bad things from happening, or make good things more likely? Or will good and bad things just happen, regardless of whether or not I worry?

◆ Does worrying really help me to cope, or does it interfere with my coping?

◆ Would I be able to handle a bad situation if I had not worried beforehand?

◆ When I am worrying, am I really problem-solving? Or am I just going over the same thoughts again and again, without finding a solution?

◆ What are the *real* effects of worrying – how is it affecting my life?

◆ How often does my worry really reflect reality? How often do I *overestimate* the likelihood of something going wrong?

◆ How often is my worrying really 'worth it'?

◆ If I stopped worrying, would it really mean I didn't care?

Use the previous questions in the following exercise. Remember that you need to consider the evidence for *and* against your positive belief about worrying.

On a new page in your notebook, write the heading:

What is my belief or thought about the positive effects of worrying?

Then write down your belief or thought.

Under this, write two new column headings: 'Proof that this belief is correct' and 'Proof that this belief is incorrect'.

Under each heading, list the evidence for and against your belief.

You have now considered the advantages and disadvantages of worrying, and weighed the evidence for and against your belief(s) about the positive effects of worrying. Based on all this information, you should be able to come up with a new, more realistic thought or belief about the effects of worrying. For example, a belief that 'If I worry, I will be more prepared' could be replaced with 'Worrying doesn't really help me prepare to deal with problems – it just makes me anxious and I feel terrible. I can deal with problems, whether I worry or not.'

Now write down in your notebook your own alternative, more realistic belief about the effect of worrying.

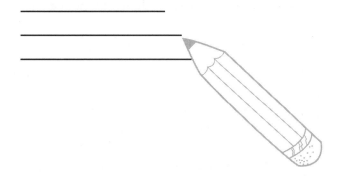

Remind yourself of this new belief whenever you find yourself worrying.

Evaluating 'old' versus 'new' beliefs about worrying

So now you have a 'new', more helpful and rational belief about worrying to replace your 'old' belief about worrying. In order to further convince yourself that your 'new' belief about worrying is accurate and helpful, you may want to try a few experiments to help you to evaluate these beliefs.

Try the exercises below and over the page to help you weigh up your old and new belief(s) about the effects of worrying.

Evaluating old beliefs

Think of a time when you worried about an approaching event, such as attending a party or going to an unfamiliar place. Now describe the anxious thoughts that you had in as much detail as possible. Include any thoughts you had about possible negative outcomes.

Next, try to recall what actually happened. Write it down.

How accurate were your worries? Were your anxious thoughts useful as a coping strategy? Write down if your worries were useful or not.

Now that you've tried this exercise with something that happened in the past, try it with a situation coming up that you are worried about. Record all your anxious thoughts before the event, and then record what actually happens. Again, you should ask yourself – how accurate were your worries? Were your anxious thoughts useful as a coping strategy?

Try not worrying!

One of the best ways to find out whether worrying is really helping is to stop and see what happens. Try the following experiment:

- For one day, keep worrying. Record what happens throughout the day. Also record how anxious you feel on a scale of 0 to 100 per cent.

- The next day, don't worry. Give yourself permission to let the worries go. Record what happens throughout the day. Also make a note of how anxious you feel on a scale of 0 to 100 per cent.

- Keep alternating days of 'worry' and 'no worry' for a week or two. Then compare your records for 'worry days' and 'no worry days'. Ask yourself: did worrying really help? How did worrying affect your anxiety levels?

If you try the exercises above, keep a record of the outcome. Use your findings to update the thought challenging exercises you have been working on throughout this section of the booklet.

8 Overcoming Avoidance and Safety Behaviours

When you feel anxious, you usually want to get away from the difficult situation as quickly as possible or do something to make the situation safer. In a truly dangerous situation, this response would be quite sensible. You would escape, or protect yourselves from danger, and the anxiety response would gradually disappear. Similarly, it would probably be useful for you to avoid similar situations or use similar strategies to 'stay safe' in the future.

Problems start when we try to escape or avoid situations that aren't really dangerous. The more we do this, the more we reinforce the idea that there is something to be scared of. In the long term, this means that we become more and more scared of things. We never discover that the situation was not that bad, or that we could have coped with it.

Safety behaviours don't make you safe!

It is also natural to want to make a scary situation feel safer. This is why people tend to use 'safety behaviours'. For example, a person who finds that parties or other social events make them anxious, might stay close to their friend or partner, or avoid saying very much, or drink a bit more than usual, or busy themselves helping out with food preparation.

Avoiding or escaping situations that trigger anxiety, or using safety behaviours to control anxiety, may make you feel better in the short term. But in the long term, the more you use these strategies, the more the fear grows, and the harder it becomes to face the situation. Each time you avoid or escape the situation or use safety behaviours, a negative message is sent. This message could be 'The only reason nothing terrible happened is because I didn't do it', or 'I got out just in time', or 'The only reason I didn't put my foot in my mouth is because I stayed next to my wife and she did all the talking'.

Over time, the number of situations that cause anxiety tends to increase and it becomes more

and more difficult to lead a 'normal' life. In order to reduce anxiety in the long term, it is important to break the pattern as soon as possible.

Identifying the problem

The first step is to work out whether you are avoiding or escaping particular situations and whether you are using safety behaviours. Ask yourself the following questions:

◆ What situations do I avoid because they make me anxious?

◆ Do I ever leave situations or activities because I feel anxious? If so, what kinds of situations?

◆ Do I have 'tricks' that I use to make me feel more comfortable in anxiety-provoking situations? If so, what tricks do I use?

To sum up, try making two lists:

1 Things that you have been avoiding, that you would like to start doing again

2 Safety behaviours that you have been using but want to get rid of

---

Asking yourself 'why?'

Very often, people avoid or escape situations because they think something will go wrong. For example, someone who was avoiding attending a party might have thoughts like 'I might get into a state and embarrass myself' or 'What if I say something stupid and everyone laughs?'

Ask yourself: 'What kinds of thoughts are leading me to avoid certain situations?' and write down your answer in your notebook.

We usually use safety behaviours because we think that they will somehow prevent something from going wrong. For example, someone who thought 'If I start talking I might say something wrong' might use the safety behaviour of not talking at a party. Or someone who thought 'No one will want to talk to me and I'll end up standing alone in a corner' might decide to use the safety behaviour of sticking by their partner or friend.

Ask yourself 'What kinds of thoughts are leading to my safety behaviours?' and write down your answer. (It may help if you ask yourself 'What am I afraid will happen if I don't use the safety behaviour?')

Avoiding situations and using safety behaviours means that you don't get a chance to find out whether your fears are justified or not. But if you challenge yourself to face the situation and get rid of the safety behaviours, you can find out the truth – which is very often much better than you expect. This can help you think about things in a fairer and more realistic way and reduce anxiety in the long term.

Evaluating the evidence

You have identified some thoughts that are making you feel anxious. Now you need to start questioning each thought – examining the evidence for and against them. Write down one of your anxious thoughts, then challenge it in the way you have done before, using the thought-challenging strategies you have already practised (pp. 14–16).

Repeat this process for each one of your anxious thoughts.

Stopping your avoidance behaviours and reducing your safety behaviours

Now it's time to test your more realistic thoughts about your anxieties by doing the things you have been avoiding and by slowly reducing your safety behaviours. When you are planning to make these changes, consider the following tips:

◆ Don't worry if you feel anxious at first when you face a difficult situation – that is normal.

◆ Take things at your own pace. Start small and work up to the really 'scary' things that you have been avoiding.

◆ You don't have to get rid of all your safety behaviours in one go – take your time and drop them one by one. It might take a while, but it will make things easier if you take it slowly.

◆ Anxiety will not disappear immediately – it will take a little while. The longer you stay in the situation, the more likely it is that your anxiety will reduce.

◆ Don't expect all your anxiety to disappear as soon as you have faced a situation once or as soon as you drop a safety behaviour. If you've been avoiding that situation or using a particular safety behaviour for a while, it will probably take time and repeated efforts to get rid of the anxiety completely. The more you practise, the less anxious you'll feel.

Boost your confidence by keeping track of your progress – write down each thing you try and record the outcome. This means that when you do something you had previously been avoiding or get rid of a safety behaviour, you should pay attention to what happens. Did the thing you fear happen or did everything turn out all right? Here is an example.

What I did	What I was worried might happen	What actually happened
I went to a party.	I was worried that I would feel nervous and end up saying something stupid, or that I wouldn't have anything interesting to say.	I felt nervous, but it was nice to see my friends. I found I had some things to talk about. I felt more comfortable as the night went on.
I tried mingling.	I was worried that I would end up standing alone and people would wonder what I was doing, or that if someone spoke to me, I wouldn't be able to think of anything to say.	I was able to talk to a few other people and I didn't end up standing all alone. I was able to talk, even though my partner wasn't there to support me.
I spoke up in a meeting and commented on someone's proposal (normally don't say anything!)	I was worried that no one would take any notice, or even worse, that everyone would look at me as if I was completely stupid.	The person doing the proposal looked a bit put out (maybe just surprised?) for a second but then said she thought I had a point.

On a new page of your notebook, copy down these column headings to make a chart for you to record your own behavioural changes, what you worried might happen, and the actual outcome.

Seeing things written down like this will help you think about things in a fair and realistic manner. But bear in mind that things might not always go well – that's life, and everyone has times when things don't quite go as they planned! But just because something doesn't go well on one occasion doesn't mean that is what it won't go well another time. Keep trying – this will help you develop confidence that you can manage situations, even when they don't go perfectly.

After you have tried a few things you had been avoiding or dropped a few safety behaviours, it might be worth going back to the thought-challenging exercises on pages 14–16 and re-doing it, using the new experiences you now have.

Overcoming your avoidance habits and getting rid of your safety behaviours will be hard work and will almost certainly make you feel anxious at times. You are, after all, changing habits that might have been with you for some considerable time, and which were designed to make you less anxious! So when you start to do things in a different way it is very likely that you will feel some anxiety, especially at first. It can take a lot of courage to stick with this anxiety. But remember: the anxiety is unpleasant but it won't harm you, and if you stick with this programme it will start to improve. So don't be discouraged! Re-read the sections you feel helped you the most and re-do some of the thought-challenging exercises (see pp. 14–16). Take pride in what you have achieved so far.

9 Staying on Top of Things

Managing anxiety usually requires quite a lot of work. Practice is important. But the hard work will pay off. Progress may be slow, especially at first, so it's a good idea to keep track of how you are doing. For example, you may want to record a daily or weekly anxiety rating (from 0 to 100 per cent) or an estimate of time spent worrying, so that you can see improvement as time passes. If you notice successes, even small ones, congratulate yourself. Remember that your thoughts are very important. Telling yourself, 'I should have done it better' or 'Anyone could do that' is unhelpful. Encourage yourself, just as you would encourage someone else.

Everyone has good days and bad days. Some days your anxiety level will be high, and other days it will be low. A task that seems easy one day may feel difficult the next. Having a 'bad day' does not mean that you're not improving or that you will never get better. Setbacks should be expected. In fact, 'bad days' can be seen as good opportunities to practise your new techniques!

Anxiety is normal and it is unreasonable to expect a completely 'anxiety-free' life – as we have repeatedly pointed out, everyone experiences anxiety from time to time, and everyone has periods when they worry too much. However, it is reasonable to try to manage anxiety more effectively and to be able to get on with life, coping with the 'ups and downs' as they come along.

Finally, it can be very useful to write down the most important things you have learned. You should also give some thought to any difficulties that you think may arise in the future and write down ideas for handling these problems. Below is a list of questions that you can use to help you keep track of your ideas. Keep your written work with this booklet, and refer back to it from time to time or whenever you start feeling anxious.

Summing up and preparing for the future

◆ What has been my most useful strategy to help manage my anxiety?

◆ Has anything else been helpful?

◆ Is there anything that I should make sure I keep doing in order to keep my anxiety levels at a manageable level?

◆ Looking into the future, are there any events or situations that might lead to me feeling anxious? If so, what are they?

◆ What should I do to help manage my anxiety in these situations?

◆ At times when my anxiety rises, what are the most important things to remember?

10 Problem-Solving

Often when people find themselves in the vicious circle of worrying and anxiety, they actually spend very little time deciding how they will solve problem. Instead, they get 'stuck', going over the same unhelpful thoughts over and over again. Making a specific and manageable problem-solving plan, and then taking action can be very helpful in reducing anxiety.

Below is a list of the main steps in problem-solving that you may find useful.

The main steps in problem-solving

◆ **Define the problem.** Instead of just going over and over the problem in your head, try to be specific. Decide what exactly the problem is and, if possible, break it down into smaller problems.

◆ **Think about your resources and list possible solutions.** Have you ever solved a problem like this in the past? Do you have any personal strengths or knowledge that might help you solve this problem? Is there anyone who might be able to help you? After you've thought about these things, sit down with a pencil and paper and write down as many possible ways of solving the problem as you can think of. Don't worry if your ideas seem silly or unlikely to work – you are simply generating ideas.

◆ **Choose a solution.** Think about the pros and cons of each solution you have listed. Think about the likelihood of success, but also consider how much time and effort would be required and how much help you would need from others. Then decide on one solution that you will try to put into action. You don't have to choose a solution that will solve the problem completely, as long as it helps you move in the right direction.

◆ **Make a plan.** Break the solution down into small and manageable steps. Make each step very specific – it should be clear exactly what you need to do and in what order. If your plan is vague or unmanageable, it will be difficult to put it into action. For example, if your solution was 'I need to get a job', your steps to a solution might include 'Get a newspaper tomorrow and review the job advertisements', 'Update my CV on Tuesday morning' and 'Make at least one application by Friday'. Make sure you decide which steps you will work on first.

◆ **Do it.** Try out your solution, even if it is only the first step to solving the problem.

◆ **Review the outcome.** If your solution works, that's great. Congratulate yourself and remember this experience for the future. If your solution does not solve the problem, review what happened. Does your plan need to be reworked or do you need to try again? Remember that, even if you haven't yet solved the problem, you are at least facing up to it – and this is likely to help you solve it in the future.

Other Things That Might Help

This booklet has provided you with an introduction to the problems of anxiety and what you can do to overcome them. Some people will find that this is all they need to do to see a big improvement while others may feel that they need a bit more information and help, and in that case there are some longer and more detailed self-help books around. Using self-help books, particularly those based on CBT, have been found to be particularly effective in the treatment of anxiety problems. Ask your GP if there's a Books on Prescription scheme running in your area – if there isn't, we recommend the following books:

Overcoming Anxiety by Helen Kennerley, published by Constable and Robinson

The Anxiety and Phobia Workbook by Edmund J. Bourne, published by New Harbinger Publications

How to Stop Worrying by Frank Tallis, published by Sheldon Press

Mind Over Mood by Dennis Greenberger and Christine A. Padesky, published by Guilford Press

Sometimes the self-help approach works better if you have someone supporting you. Ask your GP if there's anyone at the surgery who would be able to work through your self-help book with you. Some surgeries have Graduate Mental Health Workers who would be able to help in this way, or who might offer general support. He or she is likely to be able to spend more time with you than your GP and may be able to offer follow-up appointments.

For some people a self-help approach may not be enough. If this is the case for you, don't despair – there are other kinds of help available.

Talk to your GP – make an appointment to talk through the different treatment options on offer to you. Your GP can refer you to an NHS therapist for cognitive behavioural therapy – most places now have CBT available on the NHS, although there can be a considerable waiting list. Don't be put off if you've not found working through a CBT-based self-help manual right for you – talking to a therapist can make a big difference. If an NHS therapist isn't available in your area or you'd prefer not to wait to see one, ask your GP to recommend a private therapist.

Although CBT is widely recommended for anxiety problems there are many other kinds of therapy available which you could also discuss with your GP.

Medication can be very helpful for some people and sometimes a combination of medication and psychological therapy can work wonders. However, you need to discuss this form of treatment and any possible side effects with your doctor to work out whether it's right for you.

The following organizations offer help and advice on anxiety problems and you may find them a useful source of information:

Anxiety Care UK
Tel: 020 8262 8891
Email: enquiries@anxietycare.org.uk
Website: www.anxietycare.org.uk

British Association for Behavioural and Cognitive Psychotherapies (BABCP)
Tel: 01254 875277
Email: babcp@babcp.com
Website: www.babcp.org.uk
Provides contact details for therapists in your area, both NHS and private.

Mind
Tel: 0845 766 0163
Website: www.mind.org.uk

No Panic UK
Tel: 0808 808 0545
Email: ceo@nopanic.org.uk
Website: www.nopanic.org.uk

Other titles in this series

An Introduction to Coping with Depression
An Introduction to Coping with Health Anxiety
An Introduction to Coping with Obsessive Compulsive Disorder
An Introduction to Coping with Phobias
An Introduction to Coping with Panic
An Introduction to Coping with Grief (published August 2010)
An Introduction to Coping with Post-Traumatic Stress (published August 2010)
An Introduction to Coping with Stress (publisher August 2010)

If you'd like to find out more about this series, visit our website at
www.overcoming.co.uk or send an email to: introduction@constablerobinson.com.

The *Overcoming* series

The *Overcoming* series has helped thousands of people suffering from anxiety and other problems and many titles are recommended on the NHS 'Books on Prescription' self-help scheme. Subjects covered by the series include:

Anger and irritability
Anorexia nervosa
Anxiety
Anxiety in Children
Body image problems including body dysmorphic disorder
Bulimia nervosa and binge-eating
Childhood trauma
Chronic fatigue
Chronic pain
Compulsive gambling
Depersonalization and feelings of unreality
Depression
Grief
Health anxiety
Insomnia and sleeping problems

Low self-esteem
Mood swings
Obsessive compulsive disorder (OCD)
Panic and agoraphobia
Paranoid and suspicious thoughts
Problem drinking
Relationship problems
Sexual problems
Social anxiety and shyness
Social anxiety and shyness in children
Smoking
Stress
Traumatic stress
Weight problems
Worry

Order now and save money

Quantity	Title	RRP	Offer Price	Total
	An Introduction to Coping with Anxiety (pack of 10)	£29.99	**£20**	
	An Introduction to Coping with Depression (pack of 10)	£29.99	**£20**	
	An Introduction to Coping with Health Anxiety (pack of 10)	£29.99	**£20**	
	An Introduction to Coping with Obsessive Compulsive Disorder (pack of 10)	£29.99	**£20**	
	An Introduction to Coping with Panic (pack of 10)	£29.99	**£20**	
	An Introduction to Coping with Phobias (pack of 10)	£29.99	**£20**	
	Overcoming Anger and Irritability	£10.99	**£8.99**	
	Overcoming Anger and Irritability: Talks With Your Therapist (audio)	£9.99	**£7.99**	
	Overcoming Anorexia Nervosa	£10.99	**£8.99**	
	Overcoming Anxiety	£10.99	**£8.99**	
	Overcoming Anxiety Self-Help Course (3 parts)	£21	**£18**	
	Overcoming Body Image Problems including Body Dysmorphic Disorder	£10.99	**£8.99**	
	Overcoming Bulimia Nervosa and Binge-Eating (new edition)	£10.99	**£8.99**	
	Overcoming Bulimia and Binge-Eating Self-Help Course (3 parts)	£21	**£18**	
	Overcoming Childhood Trauma	£10.99	**£8.99**	
	Overcoming Chronic Fatigue	£10.99	**£8.99**	
	Overcoming Chronic Pain	£10.99	**£8.99**	
	Overcoming Compulsive Gambling	£10.99	**£8.99**	
	Overcoming Depersonalization and Feelings of Unreality	£9.99	**£7.99**	
	Overcoming Depression (new edition)	£12.99	**£10.99**	
	Overcoming Depression: Talks With Your Therapist (audio)	£9.99	**£7.99**	
	Overcoming Grief	£10.99	**£8.99**	
	Overcoming Health Anxiety	£10.99	**£8.99**	
	Overcoming Insomnia and Sleeping Problems	£10.99	**£8.99**	
	Overcoming Low Self-Esteem	£10.99	**£8.99**	
	Overcoming Low Self-Esteem Self-Help Course (3 parts)	£21	**£18**	
	Overcoming Mood Swings	£10.99	**£8.99**	
	Overcoming Obsessive Compulsive Disorder	£10.99	**£8.99**	
	Overcoming Panic and Agoraphobia	£10.99	**£8.99**	
	Overcoming Panic and Agoraphobia Self-Help Course (3 parts)	£21	**£18**	
	Overcoming Panic and Agoraphobia: Talks With Your Therapist (audio)	£9.99	**£7.99**	
	Overcoming Paranoid and Suspicious Thoughts	£9.99	**£7.99**	
	Overcoming Problem Drinking	£10.99	**£8.99**	
	Overcoming Relationship Problems	£9.99	**£7.99**	
	Overcoming Sexual Problems	£10.99	**£8.99**	
	Overcoming Social Anxiety and Shyness	£10.99	**£8.99**	
	Overcoming Social Anxiety and Shyness Self-Help Course (3 parts)	£21	**£18**	
	Overcoming Stress	£10.99	**£8.99**	
	Overcoming Traumatic Stress	£9.99	**£7.99**	
	Overcoming Weight Problems	£10.99	**£8.99**	
	Overcoming Worry	£10.99	**£8.99**	
	Overcoming Your Child's Fears and Worries	£9.99	**£7.99**	
	Overcoming Your Child's Shyness and Social Anxiety	£9.99	**£7.99**	
	Overcoming Your Smoking Habit	£9.99	**£7.99**	
	The Compassionate Mind	£9.99	**£7.99**	
	The Happiness Trap	£9.99	**£7.99**	
	I Had a Black Dog	£6.99	**£5.99**	
	Living with a Black Dog	£7.99	**£6.99**	
	Manage Your Mood: How to use Behavioral Activation Techniques to Overcome Depression	£12.99	**£10.99**	
	P&P		**FREE**	
			Grand TOTAL	

Name: _____ Address: _____

_____ Postcode: _____

Email: _____ Daytime tel. no.: _____

How to pay:

1 **By telephone:** call the TBS order line on **01206 255 800** and quote **INTRO-ANX**. Phone lines are open between Monday–Friday, 8.30am–5.30pm.

2 **By post:** send a cheque for the full amount payable to TBS Ltd. and send form to:
   Freepost RLUL-SJGC-SGKJ, Cash Sales/Direct Mail Dept., The Book Service, Colchester Road, Frating, Colchester CO7 7DW.

Is/are the book(s) intended for personal use ❑ or professional use ❑ ?
Please note this information will not be passed on to third parties.

Constable & Robinson Ltd (directly or via its agents) may mail or phone you about promotions or products. Tick box if you do not want these from us ❑ or our subsidiaries ❑.